ReKindling Your Music Ministry

ReKindling Your Music Ministry

A guide for congregations withmultiple or alternative worship patterns

Stacy Hood

Abingdon Press

Nashville

REKINDLING YOUR MUSIC MINISTRY

Copyright © 2002 by Stacy Hood

All rights reserved.

Scripture quotations are from the HOLY BIBLE, NEW INTERNATIONAL VERSION® NIV®. Copyright © 1973, 1978, 1984 by the International Bible Society. Used by permission of Zondervan Publishing House.

MANUFACTURED IN THE UNITED STATES OF AMERICA

CONTENTS

108252

Why the Music Defines The Format

It seems almost impossible to think about new worship formats without addressing the music ministry. Congregations adding a non-traditional music program or persons starting a new church with a non-traditional music ministry ask questions such as these:

Where do we begin?

- Where do we find musicians who play guitar or drums?

- Do we pay the musicians?

- How do we schedule musicians?

- Where do we find music resources?

- How do we prepare the music?

- How do we build community between "trained musicians" and "garage band musicians"?

- How do we introduce new music to the congregation?

- How do we deal with conflict among musicians?

- Once you begin to grow, how do you effectively utilize all the musicians you have?

- How do you train people to grow their gifts and abilities?

- Where do I get the answers to all of these questions?

The answers to questions about non-traditional music ministry are not yet addressed in many seminaries or graduate schools of music.

One of the first steps for congregations starting new groups in their current music ministry is to establish a positive and healthy bond between the existing leadership and the new leadership. Celebration of and respect for both traditional and non-traditional ministries is crucial for an effective and peaceful coexistence. Providing musical and spiritual growth for those in both music ministries should be of equal importance. Musical excellence and a structured program are equally important for both the traditional and non-traditional music ministry. Though the method of achieving these goals may vary, the end result will be excellent music that provides an environment for people to worship and experience God.

For those starting a new church with a non-traditional music format, the emphasis on excellence is also important. Some observers perceive that it is easier to start a non-traditional music program in a new church. While this view is accurate in many respects, there are other unique issues facing new church music ministries such as finding musicians capable of leading a contemporary program and finding and funding equipment and resources to get a program started.

One can observe several effective practices in contemporary music programs that currently exist. However, most of the examples widely available are from churches with a larger membership and staff than most churches who are interested in making this type of ministry work. All of these ministries are noteworthy and much can be learned from them, but they can seem overwhelming to a church of 250 trying to add one additional service. Though I serve at a large church (Grace Community), the structure of its music ministry might be seen as a place to start for many mid-sized congregations (100 to 1,000 members) who are attempting to worship in new ways.

Reading this book will enable you to move beyond the traditional versus non-traditional struggle to provide high-quality, life-changing ministry for all involved. A ray of hope might be found in the following chapters for those who are caught by the struggle to rekindle your music ministry. For those embarking on the new journey of a music ministry in a non-traditional setting, may the following pages hold some mind-stirring ideas to add to their own hopes and dreams. For those who have had successful traditional ministries and are exploring new worship styles, may you celebrate in what has been, what is, and what is to come for future generations.

Chapter One
Communication for Change

The decision is firm. A new worship service will be added that will look and feel different than the existing one. Many people are excited. Many are hesitant. Some are angry.

The decision to start a new church is approved. The worship service will be "contemporary." Many are excited. Many wonder if it will work. Some will never attend because it *is* "contemporary." Gathering a new group of people to work together as the Body of Christ does not happen overnight. Differing opinions of what a new church should look like along with monetary and space restrictions only scratch the surface of difficult issues facing a new church start.

Nearly every leader in a twenty-first century congregation has faced or will face some of the issues pertaining to an evolving worship pattern. It seems that people feel the need to choose sides when it comes to worship patterns. Is there any reason why both traditional and nontraditional styles cannot be seen as viable and co-existing in our worshipping communities?

The Source of Conflict

Misunderstandings and hurt feelings often lurk even after the decision has been made to add a new service. Some persons refuse to embrace the idea of new worship styles. Many individuals are tolerant, yet they disapprove of this new form of worship. Many can accept it because in their minds they "know it's not the real service, and this too shall pass."

In contrast, there are those involved in the design of the new service who are insensitive to the feelings of those who are experiencing God in the traditional service. A common misunderstanding held by the proponents of traditional worship is that those wanting change are negating what has been meaningful and relevant worship for them. Creating a new type of service is viewed as someone's judgment that the traditional service is inadequate. Immediate walls of separation can be built when those wanting a new style of worship introduce the idea in a way that appears to discredit the existing service.

Casting Vision

Clear articulation of the vision for new worship styles is the key element necessary for positive change. Change is difficult for most people. How you approach the change makes all the difference. When people are included in the process and understand the purpose, they are more likely to positively participate in the change. This process is known as vision casting.

Hours are spent in preparation and planning for a new service. A defined timeline for its implementation is successfully constructed. However, if this information is simply presented at a church board meeting with expectations that the plan will be well received, disappointment and hurt feelings may be the result. In order to promote positive change, connecting with people at their point of experience and helping them become part of the vision for the future is necessary. When people understand that new worship styles will provide another avenue for people to be touched by the love and grace of Jesus Christ, opposing views are often altered.

Providing a worship style that speaks the language of those you are trying to reach may include the use of the latest technology. Incorporating new equipment and supplies provides a means for people to participate in the creation of new worship. This creation of liturgy— whether through computer images, video, dance, paintings, music, altar design, drama, or some other media— provides people an environment in which to experience God. But the expense of new equipment or modification to current worship space will only add to the tension if its importance is not clearly defined.

Those participating in the plan for something new may see vision casting as unimportant. "Isn't it obvious that we are planning all this so that the love and grace of Christ will be shared? Isn't it obvious that we want to reach out to those who are beyond the walls of our church?" You cannot assume that this is an obvious intent or result. Nor can you assume that those persons you will draw to your service will see your vision as obvious. While people may start attending your service for different reasons, all must be involved in the evolution of the vision and growth of the church. Vision casting must be repetitive and continuous so that everyone involved remains focused on the heart and mission of the ministry.

Education as a Building Block of Support

As a member of the leadership team for one of the worship training events in my region, I spent the weekend with people sent from churches across the state to explore designing worship in new ways. Several teams were given themes and sent off to design services that would be held throughout the weekend. After leading their worship service, the design team was allowed time to share how they felt about the process of putting the service together. At the end of one service, a woman, probably in her fifties or sixties, shared these words: "I finally understand what my pastor has been trying to explain to me. This new type of worship service is not about me; it's about those people who are not here yet." That moment was a highlight of the weekend for me. This person came to the realization that adding a new worship format was not meant to discount or discredit her preferred style of worship, but rather to reach those beyond the walls of the existing congregation.

If only the hearts of every congregation could be touched in this same way! Every church currently looking to add a non-traditional service needs to identify and recruit a support team from within the current membership. Their attendance at the service is not important, but their prayers and affirmation are critical to the outcome. Questions about the new service can now be responded to with answers such as, "Yes, we are so excited to be providing yet another way for people to experience God in the life of our church!"

Just as you sometimes attend creative worship immersions at denominational or special events, you might consider creating an educational weekend for your congregation as a learning environment for vision casting. Another successful educational process for moving into the future is remembering the past. Reconnecting the congregation with its Christian roots and heritage (Wesleyan in the case of United Methodism, for example) allows them to see that stepping out in a new way to reach beyond the walls of the existing congregation is actually nothing new. (See appendix for more information on *Visual Leadership* and *ReConnecting.*) Unfortunately, many eager worship teams see the need for vision casting *after* their first attempt at implementing a new service has caused turmoil. Intentional vision casting from the beginning will save time and struggle as the plan for a new worship style unfolds. Not only does it discourage unhealthy conflict, but it is also an excellent way to remind a congregation of its purpose. With a unified understanding of purpose and direction, change can be embraced positively to continue the ministry of the church for future generations.

Fueling the Fire

Music is often the battleground for pitting traditional against non-traditional forces, and it tends to cause strife. Consider my recent experience with the non-traditional music department at an old, historic downtown church. The leadership of the church had taken steps to positively implement change and was successfully offering both traditional and non-traditional services. They have a beautiful, traditional facility, and plans are in the works for their new contemporary worship space.

During a visit with the musicians, I asked what, if any, interaction had taken place with the traditional music department. They all stared back at me with funny looks and replied that there is basically no interaction. As the discussion continued, it did not appear that either group had considered the possibility of interacting. There had been no particular situation that caused the segregation. In fact, the non-traditional group spoke of the excellent choral leadership of the traditional program. This unwritten code of separation seemed to be the assumption of both groups.

Segregated music ministries appear to be the norm among churches that have taken steps to add a non-traditional format. The pastor's message probably remains the primary, if not only, bridge between the two. The musicians lead at different services and have different rehearsal schedules. Unfortunately, there are many cases where conflict occurs, which causes leadership and participants of the traditional and non-traditional ministries to remain separate *and at odds* with each other, trapped in a simmering discontent. Often traditional and non-traditional musicians are separated from each other because neither approves of the other's ministries. This chasm *can be* and *should be* eliminated. Just as vision casting for the entire congregation is necessary, it is also necessary for the music team itself. Weeds of jealousy, competition, intimidation, and insecurity can surface quickly among musicians. Creative persons often have strong egos. Add to this an unyielding opinion of how music "should be done" in church, and more time will be spent weeding the ministry than growing it into God's instrument.

Whether you find yourself with separate ministries or planning steps to add a new service that will incorporate additional musical leadership, seeking common ground is the first step to keeping peace and promoting unity. Common ground is found when the vision and purpose of the overall ministry of the church is remembered and celebrated.

Common Ground

Whether you are a poet, novelist, or "rapper," a strong grasp of the language in which you compose will only improve your strength as a writer. Knowing more about language and its structure enhances your ability to create your own work and interpret the works of others. The same principle holds true with the language of music. Whether your musical style is classical, rock, or jazz, your understanding of the musical language only strengthens your ability as a musician. Regardless of a musician's style, practice is required to maintain and grow musical ability. Whether you sing in a 200-member traditional choir or a five-piece alternative band, you still need to vocalize for a healthy voice. Whether your worship style calls for your percussionist to play tympani for a traditional service or a drum set for a non-traditional one, the percussionist must still practice and prepare. Scales, metronomes, rehearsals, and practice are not optional in any music format.

Now take this disciplined process a bit further. As leadership in a Christian music community, we want those involved in our ministry to experience spiritual growth. We want those involved to more fully understand the gifts God has given them and live their gifts to their fullest each day. Are these desires for personal growth not a priority for any kind of music ministry? If spiritual and musical growth is a priority for music ministries in general, then use these areas of common ground to overcome issues that have served as points of segregation.

One strategy is to help all musicians see their task not only as making high-quality music, but also as anticipating high-quality ministry. High-quality music is not a goal that stands alone. The goal of a music ministry is to weave quality into the experience of encountering God. Difficulties begin when a musician or listener forms a judgment about the definition of "quality music." One example of high-quality music would be Bach in worship, while another would be a piece by Steven Curtis Chapman. Both of these men have produced superb music. Either used in a qualified manner with a heart for God will be effective, but it will reach different people. As a leader, you will recruit opinionated musicians who are for or against one composer or the other. When you put diverse musicians under the same "ministry roof," the burden is on you to prevent musical differences from becoming a stumbling block for unity in ministry.

For musicians "on both sides of the fence," communication and peaceful co-existence will not happen without constant work. The following very specific steps can be taken to promote team building among various groups of musicians in the congregation.

The Road to Peaceful Co-existence

The first step, which may sound simplistic, is to form a friendship between the leaders of the traditional and non-traditional music ministries. Perhaps the leaders of both ministries and the pastor agree to go to lunch and not discuss music. Talk about the exciting things that are happening in other ministries of the church. Discuss things you enjoy beyond music. Focus on anything that will shed positive light on the person you are interacting with. If you can form a friendship beyond music, then in the future, even if you have differing opinions, you can more easily communicate.

If the leadership can have a meal together and put aside musical differences, then you can try guiding your musicians to do the same. Have a covered dish dinner or cater a meal for both ministries. Focus once again on the exciting things that are happening in the church beyond the music ministry. Get to know each other. This might mean that a twenty-year-old college student who plays electric guitar eats dinner with the oldest member of the traditional chancel choir. "If [your] heart is as my heart . . . give me your hand."[1] Regardless of the songs they sing in their diverse worship settings, both are servants of God breaking bread together and sharing with one another in Christian community.

To make this connection, someone must take the first step. It is possible that neither music leader will be willing to initiate communication because of past conflict. In each church, different issues cause the rift between musicians. Is it the refusal of the traditional director to be open to a new style of music in worship, or is it the non-traditional director's disrespect for what has been sacred for so long that has fueled the fire? Is it the traditional director's assumption that the contemporary musician will be ill prepared, have limited musical knowledge, and sound less than acceptable? Is it the non-traditional director who will immediately label the traditional director as too stiff, too concerned with the technicalities of music, and more concerned with musicality than spirituality? If these types of issues have caused problems, it may be the pastor or other church leadership who must initiate the change and a newfound communication. *The key is to get beyond the music.* The two musicians may never agree when it comes to music, but it is hard to disagree that they are both children of God. If they understand the vision of the church and remember they are called to be the Body of Christ in ministry together, it will be much more difficult to remain at odds with each other.

During a consultation with the contemporary music ministry of a historical downtown church, I began to discuss the importance of vocalizing. I explained the difference a daily vocal routine and voice lessons could make. Recognizing that everyone could not fit private lessons into his or her schedule, I also suggested a separate time for vocalists to "work out" their voices. (This is called Vocal Aerobics at my congregation.) The group began to think about the possibilities of this training. I further suggested that this would be a great opportunity for interaction between the two music ministries: Why not invite the chancel choir members? All vocalists need a healthy voice, regardless of what style of music they might sing.

Vocal Aerobics is only one of many musical bridge-building opportunities between the contemporary and the traditional styles. Healthy and growing voices only add to the quality of both styles of music. Proper breathing, pronunciation, and control are necessary regardless of the music ministry. A music theory class is another excellent opportunity for establishing common ground. Offer a six-week beginner course for your musicians or anyone else in the congregation who is interested in learning to read music. Increasing every musician's understanding of basic note reading and chord structure could provide major growth in the entire ministry.

There are many other areas of common ground that might be found in existing programs within your congregation. A small group or spiritual growth class might be offered at a time that would allow members from both musical groups to participate. A mission opportunity might provide an occasion where both groups come together to touch the life of someone in the community. *In finding places of focus where our differences are irrelevant, positive bridges of care and respect can be built.* Looking past the music and into the eyes of another child of God can make a difference when seeking peaceful co-existence.

With vision and purpose clearly defined, a ministry can move forward into the exciting journey that God has planned. In the following pages you will find ideas and insight for creating structure and positive ministry opportunities in a non-traditional music ministry. You will also see examples of a church music ministry that is putting these concepts into practice and seeing exciting results occur.

---

1. John Wesley in Sermon 39, "Catholic Spirit." In this sermon, John Wesley uses a text from 2 Kings 10:15: "And when he was departed thence, he lighted on Rechab coming to meet him. And he saluted him and said, 'Is thine heart right, as my heart is with thy heart?' And Jehonadab answered, 'It is. If it be, give me thine hand."

Chapter Two
So You Want To Be In The Band

"We would like to have a band, but where do we get a guitar player?" asked the new music minister at First Church. The worship director at New Church down the road answered with some questions of her own: "Have you ever asked the congregation if anyone plays guitar? Why would you be interested in finding a guitar player? Would there be any reason for a person to tell you that they play guitar, especially if you have a traditional service?" A person might not see a place for their particular gift in the style of worship at a particular church. If the musician learns that a service will be added that includes new instrumentation, then you may find more people with musical gifts than you expected. As with many aspects of an unpaid servant system, you won't know until you ask.

The minister of music at reluctant Second Church counters that "We can't start the new service until we have a full band." At most startups for a non-traditional worship service, the music ministry begins with as few as four people. The playlist is short, and the band is small. Where two or more musicians are gathered, the key is to look for quality rather than quantity.

The minister of music at First Church, a congregation that serves the business leaders of his county-seat town, follows up with another old dilemma, "How many of your musicians are paid?" Well, "None," says the worship director at the growing New Church down the road. "I just do not have people in the congregation that want to play," replies the minister of music.

Some churches pay a band of professional instrumentalists to play every week. In that situation, a person might not come forward, for there is no apparent need. The leadership must clearly communicate the need for continuous growth within the music ministry. However, this focus on growth does not stem from the need to increase numbers for boastful reasons. The purpose is to increase the number of people serving in an area that utilizes their spiritual gifts.

The worship director at New Church helps the current musicians understand that participating in the music ministry *is* serving God. As she advertises for new musicians, this is made evident. This is important because people can view service as a task that they should *not* enjoy. Willow Creek writer Sharon Sherbondy addresses this in one of her dramas, *Somebody's Got to Do It* [2]. She takes a hilarious look at how some people feel they are not truly serving God unless they are miserable in the process: "If God wanted us to be happy He wouldn't ask us to serve. That's what service is all about. . . . I was brought up in the church. My father hated serving, his father hated serving. I come from a long line of unhappy servants. But somebody has to do it." The worship director reminds musicians that by doing something they love, they live their divine gift, which comes only by grace. With this understanding at the heart of the worship ministry, people enter with the attitude of servanthood, not with an attitude of volunteerism. This is a crucial shift in a ministry area that is so often associated with "performing." With servanthood understood as one of the core values, those approaching the music ministry with conflicting issues may decide they are no longer interested.

As the word spreads that you are looking for musicians who want to express a spiritual gift, new musicians actually begin to contact you! But the music director at Second Church interjects, "Now what? Being a Christian with a spiritual hunger does not excuse incompetence. How are you going to discover someone's musical ability? How are you going to incorporate these new people with the four, close-knit musicians that have been playing together every weekend for six months? How are you going to tell an instrumentalist he or she is not musically ready to participate with the band? How are you going to explain to a vocalist he or she is singing a quarter step off pitch?"

You need a process for incorporation if you are to grow a healthy music ministry that is based on a worship band format. For musicians, that process is a multi-step journey that beings with an audition. Most musicians will cringe upon hearing the term, *audition;* it conjures up failure and rejection in many instances. However, in a non-traditional worship environment, an audition may be slightly different than what you might imagine.

An Instrumentalist and Member of the Band

Wind Ensemble Auditions remain a vivid memory for me. As a college freshman, I remember how hearing the word *audition* was enough to make me hyperventilate. I was afraid of playing so poorly that the band director would simply revoke my scholarship and tell me to try another major. There were seven other horn players, and I imagined that I was in a tight race for dead last. I walked in the room shaking profusely and took my seat. I remember that there was some kind of partition separating me from the director who was judging the auditions. It was like the Wizard of Oz: "Pay no attention to the man behind the curtain." After playing my prepared piece, sight-reading another, and those dreaded scales, I was so happy to leave the room I did not care about the chair placement I might be assigned.

Most instrumentalists have felt that same anxiety through the years of auditioning for bands, as have vocalists auditioning for ensembles and solo parts. You generally make it through in much better shape than you anticipate, but the anticipation of the whole process is the worst part. Now consider your typical adult, who was fairly proficient in his or her high school band but has not touched an instrument in years. You hear that a prospect once played an instrument and invite him or her to come audition with the church group. "Don't you want to participate in this ministry?" You cannot figure out why the person does not return your call. The person, frightened off by the term audition, never looks for that bass guitar he or she once placed in jazz band.

So does this mean that you merely invite prospective musicians to come play with the band before you hear them? That would also be a mistake. An audition, a demonstration of what the person can do, is necessary. If a person wants to play bass and really does not have the necessary skills, you cannot merely invite him or her anyway and expect miraculous improvement to occur within a week or two. Instead, try wording the invitation differently. Your purpose in auditioning for participation in the music ministry is much more than testing current ability. *Your purpose is to audition their potential.* Does this person have enough musical ability, matched with a desire to respond to God's call in this ministry area, to actively participate as a team player? More often than not, persons who take a step forward are farther along than they admit to themselves.

So how do you avoid the term *audition*? Perhaps use the phrase "Jam Session" rather than *audition.* Here is one example of an advertisement for our next instrumental audition:

> *Do you play a musical instrument? Is your guitar in the back of the closet and you are not sure if you still remember how to play it? Chances are, you remember more than you think! Come jam with the band to see if you might be interested in the music ministry of_____.*
> *We are constantly looking for people who want to live their gift so that others might come to know more fully the love of Christ.*

The "Jam Session" concept immediately lets potential prospects know that they will not be auditioning alone under a microscope. In the congregation I serve, the phrase "Live the Gift" is a familiar phrase that reminds people that in this area, as in all our areas of ministry, there is an opportunity to become involved in serving by using the gifts that God has given each individual.

When people call for more information about a Jam

Session, provide them with an "Instrumental Music Inquiry" form (excerpt below) to give them basic information about participation in the music ministry as well as details about the Jam Session:

> *You will have an opportunity to play through familiar music with current members of the band. This will allow you to get a feel for the band. As you play, this also provides a chance for the band members to evaluate instrumental potential for all of the participants. Afterwards, the history of our group, our philosophy of music ministry, and the commitment necessary to be an active part of the band will be explained.*

Once a person has an opportunity to read the information and ask questions, she or he is usually ready to take the necessary steps involved in the audition journey. The player's willingness to move forward will be increased by the non-threatening nature of the Jam Session. This process is even less threatening for musicians who currently play in other venues.

On the other hand, it is often more difficult to judge true ability without a solo audition. Asking persons to sight-read a piece, play four scales, and improvise on a chord progression would certainly tell me of their immediate capability. However, *it is the responsibility of the one in leadership to be able to listen and hear the potential, not necessarily the immediate ability.* As a person in leadership, you must constantly work to improve your own ability to do this. When "auditioning" someone, *you are looking for every possible reason to include this person in ministry.* You want to listen and look for possible strengths that will allow this person to serve in the music ministry. An auditioning guitarist may not be as advanced as the three you already have. So you ask yourself whether or not you feel the person has enough skill to work up to the current musical ability level of your group within a reasonable amount of time.

During the Jam Session, move to the sound booth and listen from a set of headphones. This way, you are not standing over those "auditioning," and you can listen more intently. Also ask some of the leading musicians from the current ministry to participate in the listening process. They are the ones who are excited about incorporating new musicians, and will listen with that same attitude of "evaluating potential."

Commitment to the Vision of the Ministry

Another aspect of the Jam Session involves sharing the history of the band, the philosophy of the music ministry, and the commitment necessary to be an active part of the band. It is important for someone to understand the history of the group before becoming part of it. Equally important is for a person to understand why the group does music "the way they do it" within the context of the church ministry. If a person is an outstanding musician, yet "doesn't like the way you do things," or does not display the traits of a team player, no one will be happy. That is not to say that there is only one way to run a music ministry and your way as music director is "the way." It simply means that this is the way God has directed your ministry thus far, and you should continue to seek direction for the future. If someone feels there are issues that provoke strong disagreement, he or she should probably look elsewhere for involvement in ministry.

Another issue is the level of commitment necessary to become actively involved. Provide a commitment form outlining several things considered important for participation in the music ministry. One of the first things to expect of band members is membership in the congregation. Becoming a member at the congregation where I serve is a process called "Pathways"[3,] and a person must be actively pursuing membership in the congregation to continue the audition journey with the band. We have not had a problem with this expectation because of the emphasis on spiritual giftedness. Our membership process includes an evening with the pastors and staff, an introductory course on the history of our congregation and denomination, a class to help each person discover his or her spiritual gifts, and a class to help people grow in their spiritual journey. Once these steps are completed, a person may join the church. It is an exciting process that provides a strong foundation for involvement and for spiritual growth. There are always extenuating circumstances regarding family situations or examples such as college students who leave their membership at their home church, and we deal with those on an individual basis.

Some worship directors do take a different point of view about church membership or Christian identity for their musicians. In congregations that are thoroughly "seeker driven" or "seeker sensitive" the worship coordinator and senior staff at the church might recruit band members who are not believers as a point of entry into the congregation. To make this perspective effective, or at least consistent with the stated strategy, the church staff must intentionally work with the unchurched musician by sharing the faith and witness that is necessary to give birth to a new Christian.

Another crucial element of commitment is time. The time required for rehearsal and performance is often the deciding factor for many people who inquire about participation with the band. We are very up-front that this ministry area does require more time than most ministry areas in the life of our congregation. It is important that not only the musician, but also the musician's family, understand the time commitment. The player is also made aware that a process is in place to allow scheduling that protects a person from becoming overcommitted and burned out.

A third area of commitment involves continual spiritual and musical growth. No one ever "arrives" at a place of spiritual or musical superiority. Given the wide variety of abilities and strengths in a group, the vision of the core process of the church must be kept at the forefront—Christ, through grace, restores lives and transforms seekers to servants. This is a daily process of growth for everyone.

During the Jam Sessions, I try to recall the feeling I had as a college freshman on audition day. This is a reminder that nerves play a role in most participation in a new adventure. Though a Jam Session may initially be more work for the leadership, the benefits far outweigh the negatives of intimidation that pertain to solo auditioning.

The Next Step

If, after the Jam Session, it is discovered that some individuals are ready to begin the process of becoming team members, invite them to come to rehearsals for several weeks. This gives prospective musicians the opportunity to be exposed to some of the music used in worship, to become acquainted with many of the other musicians, and to experience the level of commitment desired. As this integration progresses, begin to look for a time to work them into the worship schedule.

One important step that occurs towards the end of a person's audition journey is to meet with a pastor and the worship director. It is not a lengthy meeting, but another opportunity to make sure the person understands the commitment required of a team member. It also allows for any questions or concerns to be discussed before bringing the person into full band membership. It may be that the person is a very capable musician, but due to situations at home or work, he or she has a problem with the time element. It may be that the person is not musically ready to continue with the team. The meeting may simply be a celebration of the person becoming actively involved. It is a positive step that seems to seal the relationship and boost it into further maturity.

Once these steps have taken place, the person should be scheduled and treated as a full member of the team. After six months, if the leadership and the musician feel that this has been a good "ministry match," the person can be asked to sign a commitment form as a full member of the team.

These steps along the way simply serve as "forced communication." Often, misunderstanding and confusion occur between individuals because people do not communicate clearly. Having clearly defined expectations and milestones promotes a good relationship between the leadership and the new person. The worship director wants all of the musicians to know that she or he cares about them as a person first and a musician second. You may have a great bunch of musicians who have all played together for a good while and have a clear line of communication among one another. However, you must be intentional as you incorporate new people to create lines of communication with them as well. They are not going to assume that you care unless you prove it.

A Vocalist and Member of the Band

The process above describes what an instrumentalist typically experiences before becoming a band member. For several reasons, the audition journey varies slightly for vocalists. The conceptual understanding of musical ability differs when comparing instrumentalists and vocalists. (You may not have experienced this problem, but it often lies beneath the surface.) My opinion is that there is a certain "internal attachment" to the voice. Though instrumentalists play from within, there is a difference with vocalists that is more subjective, and thus more indescribable: *I can sing. I want to sing. Let me sing. Why aren't you asking me to sing immediately? Are you judging my voice?* Often persons with a vocal problem are unaware, for example, that they sing off pitch. Someone may have once complimented their voice, and perhaps they have an unrealistic view of their ability. If they are told they need some vocal work, then they often view the leader as mean, jealous of their ability, or judgmental! Sometimes they feel that the leader "just does not like me." There is a level of insecurity in most vocalists that comes out in a variety of ways. Even among very talented vocalists, insecurity exists. If you are aware of the "internal attachment" factor, you will be able to more calmly address what may seem to be unreasonable behavior. (As a vocalist myself, I feel I can address this issue without being seen as an instrumentalist who is "ganging up" on the singers!)

If the only piece you could play on piano were "Chop Sticks," then you would not expect to be put in the band leading worship. However, a vocalist may not be able to hear that they have poor tone quality because their voice is either out of shape or has never been in shape. For people who have not studied music or taken voice, that "inside the head sound" seems just fine. They also may sing somewhere around the pitch instead of in the center of it and will be unable to detect this problem. This may cause the person to question why she or he is not immediately asked to participate as a vocalist in the band.

Even for someone who is vocally ready to participate, there is still a preparation period. The vocalist needs time to become familiar with pronunciations and cut-offs in the music. The person also must be ready to take constructive criticism in rehearsal. Unless you make it clear to vocalists that they will be asked to watch pitch, pronunciation, and blending, they might begin to take it personally, concluding that they are being singled out. A music director would much rather have to tell a guitarist that he or she is out of tune than tell a vocalist he or she is singing consistently flat. Training vocalists to understand that you are not condemning them when their "instrument" needs adjustment will save major heartache down the road.

Another reason that the process is different for vocalists pertains to the non-auditioned vocal ensemble or choir that may participate in a traditional or informal worship service, perhaps each week or once a month. This vocal group allows anyone desiring to participate in worship through music the opportunity to do so. When we have a "vocal advertisement" for our ministry, this is an invitation for interested singers to join us for our next adult vocal ensemble rehearsal. Anyone with an interest in vocal participation with the band is given a "Vocal Inquiry Form" and told of the next rehearsal for the adult vocal ensemble. This form clearly states that we expect anyone interested in singing with the band to participate in the ensemble as well. Anyone who is not willing to sing with the ensemble group sends up a red flag. Even the most talented vocalists need to be team players. We do not view this group as a place to "pass through" for vocalists. It is an important part of the ministry and every individual is an important part of the whole. It is so incredible every time they participate in leading worship to see the gift of music shine through them. Those who do become members of the band do not step from one group into the other, but rather participate in both.

After participating in the ensemble, the process for a vocalist wishing to sing with the band follows the same basic pattern as that of the instrumentalist. The person participates in the Jam Session experience and becomes familiar with the history, philosophy, and commitment of the group. The next step, however, is slightly different. Instead of attending three rehearsals with the band, the vocalist attends at least three vocal aerobics classes. This allows more individualized attention to vocal issues not always directly dealt with in regular rehearsals.

Instrumentalists who have been gifted with vocal ability should be encouraged to sing also. Many worship bands have a line of vocalists next to non-singing instrumentalists. This works in many situations, but allowing the musicians to both sing and play is an excellent alternative. The audition journey can be adjusted slightly for someone falling into both categories. We encourage those with the ability to sing and play to make use of both of their gifts, which goes a long way in reducing the gap between vocal and instrumental music.

The Value of the Process

When viewed as a whole, the audition journey is more than just an audition. Whether you are starting a music ministry or adding new members to an existing one, it is never too late to start a process of organized incorporation. Once a process is put into place, it should not overwhelm the leadership or the individual. The process allows someone to quickly become a member of your musical family. Many leaders of "contemporary" worship bands become so frustrated with issues that could have been avoided if clear expectations had been established. The process outlined here will not solve all your problems. People will get their feelings hurt or become frustrated, regardless of what is done to avoid it. Life is messy, but grace happens when we create a healthy environment for each member. You will always run the risk of excluding very talented musicians by not letting them "jump right in" to lead worship the week after they tell you of their ability. If a person cannot find it in her or his heart to participate in these simple steps, then she or he is probably not team player material.

A Time to Wait

What if, after someone completes a Jam Session, it is apparent the person is not ready to participate? We provide statements in our initial inquiry forms which address this issue. From the beginning, we state that if persons are not ready to continue the journey toward band membership, we will help them find ways to improve their skills. In the church we never say, "Sorry, you aren't good enough to participate with the band." For vocalists, the best tool I can provide is our free vocal aerobics class. They may also choose to study with private voice instructors, which is a plus for anyone who sings. Instrumentalists may also study with private instructors or seek help from other band members. They may also seek guidance from Contemporary Christian musicians who have recorded instructional videos. There are plenty of opportunities for someone who is willing to improve. By including these statements about lack of readiness in the Inquiry Form, persons know *before* the audition process begins how the evaluation process will work and what the expectations are. If the person is appreciative of your evaluation and is excited about growing musically, then you will prob-ably only need to put him or her on hold. There is a good chance that with practice he or she will eventual-ly become a valuable team member. Just think what pri-vate instruction and practice will do for someone who is committed to improving!

If the person is not appreciative of your evaluation, then it is not as easy for the director to work around feelings of rejection. This is another reason why the director of the group does not need to be the only person involved in the process. Other musicians, who will treat the situ-ation with confidentiality, should be involved in the evaluation. It is also helpful if a pastor, staff member, or other persons in leadership with an understanding of music can participate in the evaluation process. If not handled correctly, this process can be viewed as one person making an unfair decision. If someone has a problem, there should be input from more than one evaluator to make sure the person has not been "mis-heard."

The other crucial element that helps with making the audition process less subjective is the recording of the Jam Session. We did not do this in the beginning, but now it is always part of the process. If a person has a pitch problem or cannot come anywhere close to play-ing the music presented to them, then there is more than the opinion of those evaluating to support the case. You might view it as "hard evidence." In some cases, listening to the recording will be eye-opening for the individual who questions the decision of being "put on hold." Unfortunately, there will be those who may never hear the problem. In my ministry I have yet to encounter anyone I thought was beyond help. That does not mean, however, that they are willing to expend the time and effort to reach their potential.

Some churches have a more stringent policy for auditions than described above. Some churches state no policy at all. The audition journey is about more than music. Being a member of the band is about more than music. Participating in the music ministry allows one's self to be used so that others might experience God more fully. Participation is about using the gifts God has given us to serve in a ministry that brings about joy. It is being brothers and sisters in Christ. It is about serving, in harmony, as one body with many parts.

My scholarship was not revoked on that memorable freshman audition day. I had no idea of the incredible experience I was about to have in one of the most amazing horn sections led by a phenomenal director. What can be done by church leadership to eliminate the initial fear factor so that those gifted individuals will explore serving in an exciting, fulfilling ministry? What can be incorporated into your audition process that will allow a new musician to make a smooth transition into the music ministry? What steps can you take to help those who are not yet musically ready to become a member of the band?

---

2 Sherbondy, Sharon. *Somebody's Got to Do It* (DM 9119))(Willow Creek Community Church, 1991). This drama is available for download from http://www.willowcreek.com/.

3. "Pathways" is the name of our new member and discipleship formation process. For more information on "Pathways," go to http://www.gracehappens.org/

Chapter Three
Rotation for Life

"How many bands do you have now?" asked the music director at First Church. The response from the worship director at New Church down the road is met with blank stares: "We don't have individual bands anymore. We have a new rotating schedule that allows us to function as 'one body, with many parts.' We have a different band leading worship fifty-two weeks out of the year."

When a non-traditional music ministry reaches the point of having three individual bands, it may be time to support continued growth with a new format. Several signs suggest the direction of "thinking outside the box" as new musicians are added. The problem with three individual bands rotating three weeks at a time is that an individual musician now leads worship for three weeks and then does *not* participate in leading worship for six weeks. If the individual is on vacation with family or is sick for one of those weekends, then the time leading worship is even less. Another potential problem with this system of rotation occurs when members fill in for one another. For example, if the percussionist for the band playing the weekend service is unavailable, then one of the other band's percussionists is invited to fill in. While this seems acceptable, the musical relationship will not be as strong because those musicians rarely play together. This approach also encourages attaching labels to individual bands. "When is the 'rock and roll' band going to be leading again?" "Oh, I like it better when the 'quiet' band is leading." The bands may occasionally come together for a group dinner or meeting, but for the most part they only interact with a few members of the overall group.

These "self-contained" teams are a popular model among churches with a worship band format. This model is effective in many situations. However, as your ministry grows it may reach a point of ineffectiveness. An alternative to this model might allow you to grow your ministry beyond its current structure while enabling the growth of your individual musicians. For a new church start, this alternative scheduling process might allow a structure to be put in place in the earlier stages of the ministry, avoiding this step of self-contained teams.

A New Model for Rotation

A new process of rotation might allow you to have, for instance, twenty-five musicians and six sound techs actively rotating within the current team schedule. (This does not include those who participate with the vocal ensemble once a month.) Create a new schedule every six weeks. After carefully looking at family and work schedules, ask each individual band member to submit the dates that he or she will be *unavailable* to play during the next six-week rotation. The individual may work two weekends out of the next six. His or her spouse may be going out of town on business, which means that he or she will be handling the activities of the children at home for the weekend. A person might be planning a vacation or be aware of an extremely busy week in the near future. Once a person turns in the unavailable dates, mark those off the calendar.

There are also special circumstances to be considered for each individual. For example, one person may need to have two weeks free between each scheduled time. Another individual may have a monthly church meeting and prefer not to lead worship the week of this particular meeting. Perhaps two individuals have teenage daughters who are able to run the multimedia component of the services while they lead worship. There are times one can avoid a conflict for the members of the band in "church life" by knowing the other areas of ministry that involve the families of the musicians. This means that the worship or music director cannot be aloof or unaware of the big picture. The list of potential situations goes on, becoming part of the thought process when wearing one's "scheduling hat." We live in a busy society. Your band members have jobs and businesses they are responsible for. This type of scheduling allows people to positively incorporate serving God into their lives, with less guilt about all that God is calling them to do. However, these are only a few elements of the scheduling puzzle. Let's just say that if someone made you work puzzles as a child, it will now pay off.

After considering the schedules of team members, evaluate the information concerning the weekend services for the next six weeks. Look at how music will interact with the theme of the weekend services and which musicians will be best used for each weekend of the rotation. Some might say that scheduling this way would be impossible. It is *not* impossible. The more you work with it, the more it makes sense.

As the puzzle pieces are put into place, a schedule will be formed. Every band member will be aware of several facts when they receive their schedule. First, each member will be guaranteed to participate in leading worship two out of every six weekends. They may be scheduled more times than this, but no less. Each person is also aware that no one will play six weeks in a row. Everyone is intentionally scheduled to have a break. Rest is positive for the person, the band, and the congregation.

Once the schedule is complete, everyone will know exactly how things will take place for the next six weeks. Wrong! Life happens and the schedule will always change. Illness, family emergencies, work emergencies—you name it—will cause changes. You will already know who might still be available when someone calls with a schedule change because of the original schedules band members turned in. Other musicians will gladly fill in on short notice if they have not made other plans. You probably work with very talented and flexible people. A well-planned schedule provides the maximum opportunity for members to live their gifts. It also means that the scheduler does not take the task lightly. Scheduling should be done over several days with much prayer and thought.

Some band members may have doubts about the success of this type of scheduling. Any time you implement a change, you have to be careful to consider unexpected consequences. In the beginning the biggest question in a band member's mind might be, "Will the process be carried out in a fair manner?" "What if I don't get to play enough, or when I want to, or with whom I want to?" Though you may reassure them that the process will be fair, time is the *only* thing that will prove that the process works.

In looking back over a three-year period of fine-tuning this process, I believe that the trust level between the band members and myself, the "scheduler," is now greater than I could have imagined. They see how this process allows for a peaceful coexistence between home and service in a high-commitment ministry. They know they will be given adequate time to participate. I also believe that the members feel comfortable enough to communicate times when they need an additional break or times when they are available to do more if needed. I believe they know that I want to incorporate them into the service so that God can use them in very powerful ways: to not only touch the lives of those in worship and build more spiritual relationships with all the members of the band, but also to grow in their own spiritual journey as well.

Opposing Views

The strongest argument against this form of rotation would be one of musicality. Many directors of non-traditional worship programs are advocates of individual bands. Many would say a "groove" or a "gel" could never be achieved because you always have a different group together. Years ago I might have agreed, but after having used this process I am persuaded that musical excellence can be achieved. It may take a little additional work to do so, but it can and does happen. There are weeks when execution might not have gone as smoothly as you had hoped with the combination you scheduled. There are also weeks that are far more effective than you could have expected. This "trade-off" would be the case if the band consisted of the same seven people every weekend. With a rotation schedule, however, even more musicians learn how to function together as a team. You will have a cohesive ministry where members are on the same page with God and each other, without a battle of the bands. Every week the congregation will be led by a different combination of the musicians whom they have grown to love. Different combinations of people allow for a wide variety of musical styles, creating a unique, refreshingly unpredictable worship experience.

Patience in the Process

The scheduler (who would typically be the worship or music director) will discover that this process does take significant time and energy and is truly never "finished." There are times when I am frustrated as I complete what I consider a beautiful work of spreadsheet art and someone calls to say they are sorry, but their availability has changed. At other times musicians do not adequately check family or work commitments and must be rescheduled. This often precipitates a domino effect, changing more schedules than just one, and one has to go back to the drawing board. There are times when I fail to anticipate "cultural" issues (such as hunting season in Louisiana). If you combine the hunting population with members who are out for other reasons, you may be left with only 25 percent of the musicians available on the opening weekend of deer season. There are many things to juggle, but you learn to go with the flow while being constantly reminded that God always works it out in the end.

If you are a highly structured person you might go into cardiac arrest when working with this type of rotation scheduling. Likewise, if you are someone with no sense of structure, you could create a train wreck. The "scheduler" must see the task as an important form of ministry, and not just a menial task. I know that I am living my gift when I work on the schedule.

After the musicians become comfortable with a rotation schedule, telling them that "we are returning to the previous model of scheduling" would cause a revolt! Musicians appreciate the consideration given to their family and work obligations. Members enjoy participating with every musician in the ministry. Band members enjoy worshipping in the congregation while other members of the band lead worship. This type of scheduling allows a person to make *"Living the Gift"* a priority without sacrificing other important aspects of their life.

Finding a Good Fit

Many churches follow the distinct band approach, and it works for them. This is also a viable form of scheduling. Every situation is different, and if separate bands work best for your ministry, then continue. If you are looking for a different approach or wondering how to add musicians to the band, then I highly recommend trying your own version of the rotation process.

As the music ministry of a congregation expands, keep the "outside the box" thought process going when it comes to scheduling. Most congregations with a non-traditional worship service will have one or two other types of worship, perhaps defined by a traditional choir or keyboard music. Other churches may have two or three identical services to accommodate growing numbers and diverse schedules—one on Saturday night, and the other worship times on Sunday morning. When a person is scheduled to participate, she or he may participate in all of the weekend services. Many music directors assume there will be a distinct band for Saturday night and a different band for Sunday morning. If the worship services are different in musical style and technology, this would make some sense (but still require a lot more work for the worship director and lead staff.) If the services are identical, it would take too much time and effort on everyone's part to change out the band from Saturday night to Sunday morning. Very few band members have a problem with participating in worship two days, because they are not scheduled every weekend.

As we add new types of services, we will adjust scheduling practices once again. What will not change is the consideration given to each person, the needs of the service being scheduled, and the unity of the ministry.

Chapter Four
Team "Works"

After surviving my college freshman audition, the moment of the first rehearsal arrived. No one bothered to inform me that all those upbeats I played in my small high school band were about to be few and far between. Suddenly I was thrown into the powerhouse section of my college wind ensemble. Not only were there eight horn players, but the top two horn players were also the top two upperclassmen music majors of the school. They were intense, and I was placed right between them! They landed the top two chairs of the horn section—first and third, and I had been placed second.

The moment came for the first downbeat, and it was all horn. I do not remember the piece, but the entire section had the opening chord. We began, and the conductor stopped immediately: "Everyone has to play!" The downbeat was given once more, and we were cut off in the first measure. "Everyone has to play at the beginning of the chord. Stacy, you have to play at the same time everyone else does." I had started my note a fraction of a second after everyone else to make sure I would land on the correct pitch. I could not imagine that anyone would notice with so many of us playing. At the time I wanted to crawl under my chair, but that moment was the beginning of my understanding of how important the team is to musical success. Every single person sitting in that room was important to the conductor. Not just from a musical standpoint but a human standpoint. We each had an important role to play, and our conductor wanted to bring out the best in us.

The two upperclassmen music majors took me and the other freshman under their wing. They not only interacted with us during rehearsal; they also became our friends. This friendship was vital to our success as a horn section. The conductor, private horn instructor, and other music faculty instilled in these upperclassmen the desire for musical excellence. They transferred this desire to yet another incoming class. The model of team building and friendship also transferred. In essence, my horn section was my "small group" in the music department.

Promoting Unity

The dynamic of team building and community is even more important in church music programs. Everyone will not automatically understand that their individual gift makes a huge difference in the life of the whole group. The leader's ability to see potential does not guarantee that the individual will see with the same eyes of faith. If you do not remind individuals of their importance in the team, insecurity and doubt can creep into their thought process. The leader cannot assume that a group of similarly gifted people will automatically become "one big happy family." Relationships must be intentionally formed and strengthened to allow a team to grow beyond its current state. Celebrating the uniqueness of each individual, learning to love one another as Christ loves, and connecting the individual with the group are priorities. This will allow the *light of Christ* to be evident in the ministry. If intentional steps are not taken to promote team building within a music ministry, you risk jealousy, miscommunication, and musical mediocrity. This is true of any group, but *especially* musicians. (I can say that because I am one!)

Musicians bring a variety of musical experiences to a church music ministry. Many pianists never played in a high school band. They have performed at recitals, festivals, and private lessons. Many band students have never studied music with a private instructor. String players have played in orchestral situations, but they may have never experienced a marching band. Some musicians have never played in a conducted group. Many musicians read "the dots" while others read only chords. Many vocalists come with choral training while others have excellent voices with no formal training. Put all of these elements together in the same "musical mixing bowl," and it can take time and effort to blend. These are only a few elements one might encounter. Also added to the mix are the individual personality traits of each musician. Scary, isn't it? Intentional time must be spent beyond the music to make the music department work.

Team Building Strategy

Some would stop at this point and say, "It is hard enough to get people together for rehearsal and worship, much less take time to do anything else." This is a valid perception. Creativity is the key to finding your groove with the team. My ministry area prays together, plays together, and eats together! *Food is a key element for successful team building.* More team building has taken place over pizza and Mexican food than any other activity. Next to their hunger to serve God, musicians share the desire (and need) to eat!

On rehearsal evenings, most church musicians are either rushing in directly from work, or from hauling their kids back from after-school activities. Rather than having everyone inhale food in the car, designate times for everyone to bring his or her favorite fast food, and begin rehearsal by eating *together.* Ordering pizza is another excellent idea for a quick food solution. A meal of yogurt or salad might be more appropriate for those vocalists who do not want to sing after a full meal. Find what works for your group. Yes, this may start rehearsal a little late, but how many music ministries that work with a full staff of unpaid servants really do start rehearsal on time? While eating, you can share prayer concerns and discuss the service for the weekend. You incorporate the "small group" aspect into your ministry and everyone is fed at the same time. It is truly a "happy meal!"

Eating together is not something to do every week. Look for times when the rehearsal schedule will allow for it. Incorporating meals together simply requires planning ahead. One particular summer those of us in the band for the weekend met before rehearsal at a cafeteria down the street. This provided another time and place for strengthening the team dimension of the ministry.

Some of your musicians probably have the gift of hospitality. Which of them can become the food coordinator? I recently worked with a group that had a vocalist who was extremely excited about taking on the task of coordinating food for the music ministry. It was another spiritual gift that she could practice through the music ministry. We have a member of our band who stops at the donut shop on Sunday morning when she is on rotation. The gift of hospitality she brings to that early Sunday morning hour makes a huge difference in the life of each person involved.

Gathering musicians together with their families is another key element involved in team building. We rented a jumping machine and put it in the worship area for one of our family gatherings. The nursery workers and the kids had a great time. As nursery workers played with the kids, the adults were able to interact with each other. It was another way to say, "we care about you and the members of your family." This gathering also allowed the musicians and each of their families to become better acquainted. Incorporating the whole family speaks loudly about how much you value the participation of the team member. The spouse and/or children understand that even if they do not play a musical instrument, they are an important part of the team.

Bowling is another excellent team-building event. Take a rehearsal evening and go bowling. It does not matter if anyone can bowl! The point is to build relationships and have fun. A mission project is another idea for team building. For our Christmas party this year, our entire Worship Related Ministries team and their families helped a nearby community with neighborhood improvements. Together, we made a difference in the life of this community. The collaboration made a difference in the life of Worship Related Ministries as well.

Strong Teams Make Better Music

Team building makes a musical difference. *People who understand each other and care about each other have a much harder time "copping attitudes" with each other.* Take the sound system, for instance. Rehearsals become painfully long when no one is happy with the monitor mix. The mix gets louder because "I can't hear myself!" As it gets louder, each person complains to the sound tech until everyone is sufficiently unhappy with the mix. Then the announcement is finally made that, "we are going to have to deal with what we have and rehearse". A monitor mix is not supposed to be about how loud "I" can be; it is about how blended "we" should be. "I" does not need to overpower the "we." Everyone needs to be heard so that musical excellence is achieved. When you *know* the musicians in your band, and you are true *friends* with these people, sub-liminal messages (*like "The sound tech does not like my voice so that is why I cannot hear" or "I'll say my monitor is fine, but really I cannot hear, and I do not understand why no one cares about me."*) that creep into the musi-cian's mind tend to cease. When the band functions as a team, *everyone* will want each person's mix to be pleasant. When the sound tech is treated as the most important *instrumentalist* on the team, the entire mind-set changes. Musicians and sound techs are on the same team, not struggling for advantage over one another. Think about the time that might be spent rehearsing if mixing monitors were simple and stress free. With some monitor guidance and team building, you can greatly reduce this painful time in your rehearsal. There will be times when you run into problems with monitors, but occasional difficulties are easy to manage in comparison to a weekly war over the sound system.

Without team building and effective communication, you will cultivate a weed-infested band (or even choral group) that chokes on its personal insecurities. Have you ever met the following musician? Have you ever become this musician?

> *I wonder why that person was picked to sing this week's special instead of me? I bet the director doesn't think my voice is as good as that other person. You know, come to think of it, I was scheduled three times last rotation and that person sang four times. I bet the director really doesn't even like me! What if no one on the team likes me?"*

An innate level of insecurity can easily creep into a musician's thought process. This mental reaction is normal. However, someone who feels valued and affirmed in his or her contribution will pull up those weeds that choke their gift. Whether singing the lead or the background vocals, each person is an important member of the team. For instance, one of our percussionists played an "egg shaker" in the middle of a song, and it was an awesome moment. The moment was not only experienced, it was celebrated. Members of the team shared spontaneously what a difference the seemingly small part had made in the musical effectiveness of the piece.

When people are focused on the importance of each individual within the whole, the mindset changes. Team building provides a foundation for musicians to work together in a supportive environment. As the leader, finding ways to build your team is one of your main responsibilities. You must be very intentional about creating a cohesive group and constantly look for ways to achieve this. Once trust and communication are established among team members, the door is open to unlimited possibilities. Are there those in your ministry who can organize team-building events? What can you do to remind the members of your team that each individual is an important part of the whole? Who will bring donuts Sunday morning?

Chapter Five
Reaching Higher

The beginning efforts of team building in the music ministry of my congregation were proving to be successful. Musical strength, spiritual growth, and positive attitudes were prevalent. Worship each weekend was wonderful. So what was the problem? Why "rock the boat?" Part of the responsibility of leadership is to look beyond where the ministry is at the immediate moment. Once again, leadership requires vision casting. I did not want our ministry to become lost in our accomplishments thus far, as God had much more in store for us. I did want us to find ourselves wandering in the desert...

Excitement was in the air when the Israelites were delivered from Egypt and headed toward the Promised Land. However, at the first hint of problems, the Israelites were ready to pack it up and go back to their old way of life. As the Egyptians approached, the Israelite response was, "It would have been better for us to serve the Egyptians than to die in the desert!" (Exodus 14:12b) Moses replied,

> "Do not be afraid, Stand firm and you will see the deliverance the Lord will bring you today. The Egyptians you see today you will never see again. The Lord will fight for you; you need only to be still." (Exodus 14:13–14)

Pharaoh and his army drowned in the sea as soon as the Israelites passed through safely: "And when the

Israelites saw the great power the Lord displayed against the Egyptians, the people feared the Lord and put their trust in him and in Moses his servant" (Exodus 14:31).

Once they were past this crisis, the Israelites again forgot their "trust in the Lord and his servant." They grumbled about water, yet God provided. They grumbled about food, yet manna and quail were sent. What if Moses had done more intentional team building activities with the Israelites? Might they have had more faith in the vision God was sharing with him? Communication was not Moses' gift, and so his dependence upon Aaron. Obviously, Moses tried to follow God's plan; but one wonders whether additional time spent on casting the vision would have reduced the numbers of grumbling Israelites.

Looking beyond the immediate ministry moment and casting vision for the future is crucial for those involved in leadership. Equally important is the responsibility of the leader to *connect* the team members to the vision of the future. A God-inspired plan will seem irrelevant if ownership is not given to the team. Staff members are to be frequently reminded that the goal is to be "under" ministry areas, not "over" them. With this thought process as the focus, providing a foundation on which people can participate in life-changing ministry is a priority.

We still live with the Israelite "Desert Syndrome." When we encounter certain situations, we often panic first and later remember that God is guiding us the entire time. If we are not clear of our purpose and path, grumbling, negativity, or simply disinterest can set in. When our music ministry reaches a new place of comfort, if the desert can be described as a comforting habitat, I intervene so that we do not find ourselves in the desert too long. The leader's job is to keep moving towards the next step God has in store for our ministry. So one evening we began on a journey to new ground . . .

Taking It to the Next Level

One evening, our entire team of instrumentalists, vocalists, and sound techs gathered together. Balloons were a specific part of the décor, as they would become a key visual later in the evening. After a wonderful dinner, cooked by one of our spiritually-gifted chefs, workbooks were passed out to each member of the team. They were encouraged to open the book and read the first page. They found the following:

> A bouquet of balloons is a beautiful sight. Children's eyes light up at the sight of a clown holding them at the fair. High school students are thrilled when they receive them at school. The festivities are made complete at any party as they float around the room. Balloons are individually beautiful, but their beauty is only enhanced as a group.

> As the first balloon loses air, the whole bunch begins to lose their flair. It only takes a few drooping balloons to make the whole bouquet unable to float as high as it once did.

As a team we are similar in many ways to a bouquet of beautiful balloons. When we are "floating" together as a group, full of "air and energy," we are a beautiful sight. However, when one or more of us "loses air," it is more than an individual situation; it affects the whole team. We can look at this from many aspects of the team, but specifically we want to think about it musically. When one of us rushes the tempo, plays a wrong note, or sings an incorrect harmony, it affects the whole team. Our overall musicality is decreased because we are "floating" lower than our potential.

So does this mean we take out the balloons from our bouquet that do not float at maximum height? Absolutely not. We have an opportunity to continually "refill our helium." Even the best musician on the team will continue to make mistakes, but as we take time to practice and to fill ourselves with knowledge, our own personal balloon will float higher each week. We will learn to overcome problems that challenge us musically and find a new sense of musical freedom that we have never felt before. Not only is this beneficial for us personally, but our fulfillment as a member of the team is also increased.

You have heard the phrase, "You can lead a horse to water but you can't make him drink." In the same sense, I can provide the helium for your balloon, but I cannot force you to use it. It is part of my responsibility as a leader to provide ways for you to grow as a musician. I cannot force you to use the tools or suggestions I provide. However, I can assure you that it will be a specific part of my prayer life that you will agree to join me on this journey to *The Next Level*.

This particular evening was the beginning of an educational focus for our music ministry that has come to be known as "Taking It to the Next Level." This phrase never loses its meaning as the focus is always on growing into all that God would have us be. Though the whole evening was something God was guiding, it was a tense evening from a leadership standpoint. Many of the issues covered that evening had never been addressed with the entire team. I knew no one would disagree with the idea that spiritual growth is an important part of the journey, but I also wanted to stress the importance of musical growth as well: A combination of spiritual and *musical growth* allows us to be more *fully used* by God and *more fulfilled* in our call to ministry. Musical growth . . . ?

As we moved through the workbook we looked at things that hinder musical growth. *Unrecognized need* tops the list of barriers: "Don't we sound fine the way we are?" In church, "music education" is often seen as unnecessary. Unfortunately, it is often the "contemporary" programs that shun music education the most. *Time* is also an issue for everyone. "I need to spend more time practicing than the time spent at rehearsal?" (Many people view *practice* and *rehearsal* as one in the same.) However, *fear and sensitivity* as barriers to growth often need the most attention. Thus, the next section of the workbook:

> We, the artistic types, are sensitive. Let's try that again. WE, THE ARTISTIC TYPES, ARE SENSITIVE. It is hard for us to be told we are playing or singing (especially singing) a wrong note. We tend to take it personally. Now add to that frustration someone telling us we are off and we, ourselves, cannot hear or feel that we are off. Put all of this together and *more often than not we get our feelings hurt.* Then we find ourselves defensive and shrink back musically. Why? Because deep down, we are afraid of failure and embarrassment.
>
> We must constantly work to "depersonalize" steps to musical growth. If someone told me I had worked an algebra problem incorrectly and showed me the correct way to work the problem, I would not take it personally. It would not hurt my feelings in the slightest. Of course, I cannot stand algebra and would not put my heart into it if you paid me. *We love music and put our hearts into it.* We also use music as one of the ways to serve God. We have a tendency to regard "instruction" about what we are doing as mere criticism of our attempt to use our gift for God. We have to make a conscious effort to reverse this train of thought. Comments

and critique from someone need to be viewed as coming from a person who walks beside you to build you up, not one who pushes you down the hill. *Note: I am not promoting that we all start "sharing" with each other what we do wrong each week, and make it our mission to start keeping lists of everyone's mistakes. We must be open in rehearsals to basic critique and changes, but individual growth comes from working with someone you trust and from being honest with yourself about your own strengths and weaknesses.*

To become better musicians, we should decide to be open enough to grow. This means being open enough to learn new skills, techniques, and ideas. As much as I love voice lessons every week and would not give them up for anything, there is always the part of me that feels inadequate every time I walk through the door. For example, these are the kind of thoughts that run through one's head:

"I know I'm not as good as his young vocal majors. I don't know why he puts up with me. I know he must wonder why anyone gives me a microphone when he works with so many talented voice majors. I know when my voice cracks on these vocal exercises it must hurt his ears. I know I look like an idiot when I do all these breathing things. I know no one else looks as ridiculous as I do. . . ."

These thoughts are continually in the back of my mind even while I have a voice lesson, learning something new and having a good time each week. Barry Green talks about this problem in his book, *The Inner Game of Music*, which he co-authored with Tim Gallwey.[4] He writes:

"If you think about it, the presence of that voice in your head implies that someone or something is talking (it calls itself "I"), and someone or something else is doing the listening. Gallwey refers to the voice that's doing the talking as "Self 1," and the person spoken to as "Self 2." Self 1 is our interference. It contains our concepts about how things should be, our judgments and associations. It is particularly fond of the words "should" and "shouldn't" and often sees things in terms of what "could have been."

Self 2 is the vast reservoir of potential within each one of us. It contains our natural talents and abilities, and it is a virtually unlimited resource that we can tap and develop. Left to its own devices, it performs with gracefulness and ease.

The rule given in their book states: "If it interferes with your potential, it's Self 1. If it expresses your potential, it's Self 2 (p. 17)."

Eloise Ristad considers these voices our "judges" and writes:

Experiment for a moment. Close your eyes and look at your own private collection of judges. You will find these shadowy characters rather easily. They are the figures of authority who impose heavy rules upon you—who send you off on endless missions of duty rather than let you know what you really want and need. They are the ones you keep trying to shove out of the ragged edge of your consciousness, but that hang on with the obstinacy of spoiled children. They are the ones who give you that vaguely uncomfortable feeling in your gut when you don't measure up to their invisible yardstick . . ." (*A Soprano on Her Head*, p.14.)[5]

Eloise's words remind me that we, more often than not, perceive many people in life as judges who are not really judges at all. We let ourselves listen to the interference in our minds: he must think *this*; she must mean *that*. We only contribute to our fears when we allow "Self 1" to get the best of us. Who or what do we allow to interfere with our God-given gift? Are we willing to work to put aside the voices in our heads to grow musically in God's Kingdom? Does it help to know you are not the only person who struggles in this area?

I waited anxiously as everyone took time to digest this proposal. A sticky issue had been openly addressed with the entire group, so behind my enthusiastic smile much prayer was taking place! As people began to respond, the mood was incredible. One of the first responses was in reference to comparing musical critique to that of an algebra problem. This one example put "criticism" in a whole new light. Musical growth began to take on new meaning for the team. They began to understand music education as a tool to enhance God-given gifts. *It was as if permission had been granted for everyone to be comfortable enough to admit that they had room to grow.* No one had ever suggested that growth should not occur, but the underlying fear factor had subliminally made everyone want to shove musical mistakes and musical "unknowns" under the carpet. Now, instead of skipping unfamiliar chords, people ask openly about chords they do not know so that they can learn them. Instead of shying away from a melody or harmony line, people openly ask for help. "Ask and it will be given to you; seek and you will find; knock and the door will be opened to you" (Matthew 7:7). It applies not only spiritually but also musically.

This evening of "Taking It to the Next Level" was a pivotal point in our music ministry. Before a sense of arrival or satisfaction could set in, a vision for the future was cast and ownership by the group was claimed. Intentional team building served as a form of prevenient grace; it was the key factor allowing "taking it to the next level" to become a reality.

Our diversity stays intact. We will never all think alike or be free from disagreements. There will still be wrong notes played and occasional "squeals" in the sound system. However, we encounter these issues standing together as One Body in Christ.

A Plan of Action

Once everyone becomes open to growing his or her gifts, the leader moves to the difficult task of encouraging musical growth. Such growth cannot be proposed and left to individuals to attain on their own. A few team members may study music privately, but the possibility of everyone on the team taking private lessons is unrealistic. It is important that high-quality opportunities be provided for the group so that musical growth might not only occur, but also be a joyful, team-building experience.

Since 98 percent of the team participates vocally, we start with the voice. For the vocal seminar we included our adult band vocalists, our adult vocal ensemble, and our youth band vocalists. Out of the entire group, there were no more than five people who have ever studied voice privately. Though everyone in our program is exposed to vocalizing and proper vocal technique, this adventure was going to be very different for many people.

Some vocal coaches work with church music programs. At my congregation, we hired Chris and Carole Beatty. They do seminar work with churches and at music festivals around the country. They also have a studio outside of Nashville where they do private coaching. There are highly qualified instructors in our community, but sometimes bringing in someone from outside the local context can make a huge difference.

From the moment Chris and Carole began, they captivated the entire group. The day was a huge step forward for our vocal ministry. Even our youngest youth could relate to their method of instruction. They are very serious about what they teach while maintaining a very fun and active style. The Beatty's have an incredible teaching style that celebrates the voice as an important God-given gift while working to enhance it with proper technique. They place much importance on proper care for and growth of the voice. In one day we witnessed their incredible ability to attain vocal quality beyond the expectation of most individuals. The sound of the entire group at the end of the day was phenomenal. The Beatty's training, partnered with the foundation previously laid by the leadership of our music ministry, provided a new level of vocal growth.

Our connection with Chris and Carole has gone beyond this one-day seminar. They carry a complete line of Vocal Coach resources designed to provide guided workouts for both individuals and groups. CDs, videos, and cassettes are available, covering a wide range of topics. There are specific workouts designed for warming up and working out ensemble groups, as well as workouts targeted for individual voice types. Workouts for specific target areas such as tone, breathing, and range expansion are also available.

Think about the vocalists in your group. How incredible to be able to provide a high-quality resource for them to exercise their voice on a daily basis! This is not a substitute for private voice lessons, but it is one of the best alternatives I have discovered. Ensemble resources like these can also provide new exercises to add to your current rehearsal warm-up routine. Even if you, as a music leader, have never had vocal training, the Beatty's series of resources is easy enough to use so that you can move your vocalists to a new level of musicality.

After a very successful venture with the Beattys, we continued the educational process. We brought in instructors to work with our instrumentalists. We have established someone locally to provide additional training for our sound techs. Our last workshop was with Will Denton, the current touring percussionist for Steven Curtis Chapman, Erin O'Donnell, and Mark Schultz. Will spent the day with a "circle of drum sets" in our worship area with our entire youth and adult percussion sections. Denton's great respect for musical excellence, matched with a heart for God, provided an incredible "next level" step for our percussionists.

It is important to balance these larger training events with musical growth opportunities provided by one's own music staff. Provide short-term music theory opportunities for those who are willing to spend extra time increasing their knowledge of the music language. Provide a vocal aerobics class to enhance vocal technique. Encourage "sectionals" by having all of your guitarists gather once a quarter to work on new music. In a rotational scheduling process, all of the instrumentalists in one section will not be leading worship together at the same time. Sectionals allow them to stay connected and ask questions pertaining specifically to their instrument. Review video footage of worship services. Celebrate the successes and learn from the mistakes. All of these types of opportunities can be woven into a strong foundation of music education.

Growing Leadership

The "Taking It to the Next Level" emphasis provides growth for the individual team members and the team as a whole. It also provides opportunity for new leadership to emerge within the music ministry. In order for a ministry area to grow beyond what one person can adequately juggle, more leaders must be identified and recruited.

Another lesson can be learned from the leader in the desert. As the Israelites' time continued in the desert, Moses' father-in-law, Jethro, came to visit. He celebrated with Moses as they reflected upon all God had done during their amazing journey. However, after spending some time with Moses, he shared some very valuable information. He pointed out to Moses that he alone was trying to meet the needs of all the people. In modern terminology, Jethro basically told Moses he would reach burnout if he did not establish teams of people to carry out the ministry. *Find those who can be trained as leaders and get them involved. You are not supposed to be doing this on your own!* Jethro helped Moses see the importance of team building.

"Jethro's Wisdom" is another piece of advice frequently reiterated to the staff at my congregation. Just as Rob Weber reminds staff to be "under" ministry, he emphasizes that ministry is not something to "do" alone. We are constantly challenged to re-evaluate how we can more effectively incorporate additional leaders to carry out ministry. If we fail to do this, we only stifle ministry. For our music ministry, the "Taking It to the Next level" focus provides opportunity and growth to allow leaders to be formed.

When I received a phone call requesting that one of our bands lead worship for a conference event, the first thought that popped into my head was, "I cannot fit one more thing into this next month. There is not enough time to get this together, and too much is happening for me to be out of town that weekend." Then, I immediately stepped back from that thought and regrouped. There was no reason "I" needed to be present. This particular event was for upper high school and college-age students, and we had a great group of musicians in this very age group. We also had a very capable leader within our music ministry who could take these students to this event, allowing a great ministry opportunity for all involved. By refocusing my thoughts, ministry was enabled, not stifled. With intentional growth opportunities available, more capable music leadership will emerge out of a ministry area.

The importance of the "Taking It to the Next Level" emphasis is multi-faceted. Growth of individuals, the group, and emerging leaders takes place while the excellence of the music itself increases. All of this takes place within the context of the vision of the core process of our church: Christ, through grace, restores lives and transforms seekers into servants. With the emphasis on growth being not only spiritual, but musical as well, the ministry area provides a well-balanced group of people living their gifts!

4. Gallwey, Timothy, and Green, Barry. *The Inner Game of Music* (Doubleday, 1986).
5. Ristad, Eloise, *A Soprano on Her Head* (Real People Press, 1982).

Chapter Six
The Ritual of Rehearsal

Ever had a worship nightmare? In my nightmare we are worshipping in a mall and all the musicians decide to go shopping right before the service starts. One dream included the entire worship service being moved outside right as the service began, and I could not find the congregation. The most recent nightmare involved shag carpet in the worship area! Most worship nightmares include problems with the projection system because nothing was typed into the computer. My latest nightmare included one of our soloists showing up in a green prom dress from the '80s. Ridiculous!

When do worship nightmares actually occur? Typically between Thursday night rehearsals and the weekend services. Worship nightmares provide me with stress relief. There is often that struggle after rehearsal when you know that things did not go as you had planned; yet you know that when everyone returns and works a little more on the music that it will all come together. When a worship nightmare occurs, I am reminded that things could be much worse! A real service will never have nearly the problems my worship nightmares propose.

For me, rehearsals are highly stressful situations. Much of the stress is self-imposed. I find rehearsals stressful because they involve so much more than the music; yet in the end, quality music is the expected outcome. *Though weekend worship services are the culmination of all the work that goes into a music ministry, rehearsals are the place where the spirit and readiness of the team is built.*

When musicians arrive for rehearsal, they have already spent an entire day at work. Do not take their state of mind for granted. Yes, they have made the commitment to be there and have it scheduled as part of their lives, but always keep in mind that rehearsal needs to be as fun and stress-free as possible so that there is joy in "Living the Gift."

Incorporation of small-group time and prayer are crucial. It does not always go as planned, but this kind of spiritual connection should be present in some form each week. It may be five minutes or thirty minutes, depending on the dynamics of your group on any given day. Varied opportunities for spiritual growth in the group can be imagined. You may use worship journals, allowing the band to use the pastor's upcoming worship theme in their devotional time. You might provide a book for everyone to read and discuss at rehearsal; or you might know that a large percentage of your musicians are involved in studies currently offered, so you do not have a structured study for the group. The important thing is to stay in tune with what is needed year round. Offering different opportunities for spiritual growth throughout the year helps keep any one ritual from becoming routine. Prayer, however, never loses its power!

The fact still remains: Quality music is the expected outcome for a music ministry. How do you effectively use your rehearsal time to allow this quality to surface? Once again, you must look beyond the music.

Prayer and preparation serve as the foundation upon which a successful rehearsal is built. With this as the basis, there are several steps that can keep those "worship nightmares" far from the realm of reality.

Keys to Successful Rehearsing

Several key elements make the rehearsal a success. First, having your most important band member present is crucial: the sound tech. From a leadership standpoint, I would rather give up any one musician in the set before having to rehearse without the sound tech. Dealing with sound system problems is painstaking. If you pull a sound system out of a closet each week, this adds further stress to rehearsal. Even a nice sound system in a space designed for a band produces problems on occasion. Musicians tend to get edgy when dealing with sound issues. Sound techs and musicians must have mutual respect for each other. The sound system should be "ready for take off" before rehearsal to promote positive communication. If chords are run and channels are marked, then mixing monitors for rehearsal is a matter of a few stress-free minutes rather than an extended period of frustration.

The next key to a successful rehearsal is advanced music preparation. In my situation, I have someone who "lives his gift" each week by preparing music folders for rehearsals. The music is in order and on the stand when the musician arrives. Usually, if new music is being learned, the musician will receive the music before rehearsal. There are times when music might change on short notice or a new song is added at the last minute, but these quick changes are easy to deal with because of the standard preparation that is in place.

The third key to success is avoiding the "run through" syndrome. The music for the week is familiar, and you run through it once and move on. This rut is easy to fall into. When you are preparing music that is very familiar to the team, discuss the sections in the music that tend to cause a recurring problem or that have difficult rhythmic patterns. Talk through intros and outros as they will work in the particular format of the worship service. This is extremely important for a group that rotates through different musicians in the band each week. As the director, you must intentionally ensure that everyone is on the same musical page. Adjustments to music as it becomes part of your repertoire must be conveyed to the entire team. Properly marked music and communication help to avoid the "run though" syndrome.

A fourth key to a successful rehearsal is the tempered used of digression. It can happen at any moment of a rehearsal. My typical response is: "Moving along, before we digress any farther!" However, I was once drawn into a lengthy digression myself. It happened in the middle of rehearsal; the guitar player started it. A familiar tune was quickly picked up by the bass player, and four bars later by the drummer. The music did not stop until the vocalists finally made it to the point where no one could remember the rest of the words. In hindsight, it was quite humorous. I must admit I let the digression go on much longer than normal because it was one of my favorite songs. That particular evening, however, the digression made a positive difference in the endurance of those rehearsing. We had a very difficult special piece of music planned for the weekend, and I knew the rehearsal would be lengthy. By allowing a moment of extended digression on a classic, familiar song, any tension that might have been lurking was reduced. We then moved on to successfully preparing a new piece for the weekend.

Knowing when to allow digression is important. I realize many other factors, such as prayer, preparation, and skill were the real reasons the music was learned that evening. I also know short moments of digression go a long way toward keeping joy and friendship alive in the rehearsal. Putting the elements together at the right time creates a successful rehearsal environment.

The Tension of Time

One of the first "professional gigs" I ever played was as a senior in high school; the youth orchestra was scheduled to perform with the local symphony. Members of the youth orchestra were not paid, as this was simply an opportunity to participate in a learning experience. As we all took our places at the rehearsal, a very serious-looking person walked in with a very, very large clock. He placed the clock on a music stand and left the stage. The rehearsal began. The clock was important for everyone involved. As a professionally paid musician you are expected to be on time and to be prepared. As the conductor, the same is expected of you. When the time allotted for the rehearsal is complete, the rehearsal is ended. Any addition to the rehearsal schedule is considered overtime.

From this experience I moved to the rules of a college rehearsal schedule. You arrive early and are prepared or your grade is lowered. Rarely did someone walk into the rehearsal late. If someone did, you wanted to crawl under a chair for the person. The conductor meant business when it came to time.

These experiences instilled in me an understanding and appreciation for the issue of time. This rigid adherence to time forces you to respect the life of each person involved. Sticking to the schedule also makes sure that the time planned for a task will be preserved.

In my current situation, I am now the one responsible for the rehearsal. There is no pay to be docked or grades to be lowered. This is the case for many church music programs. You have people who are early and prepared and people who are habitually late. As the "conductor" you are responsible for providing a pleasant and timely rehearsal, yet you have no control over early or late arrivals. Although I will never give up on educating musicians that part of their responsibility is to be prompt, I must not allow the issue of time to interfere with the success of the rehearsal.

The mindset of a director in the church setting often has to move from watching the clock to being the clock. If you are behind schedule, you must take the time you have and make it adequate for the task at hand. While warming up with a particular piece of music, you might have to quickly re-work the entire rehearsal in your mind. If you know your musicians and the music, then you reflect a time frame and a plan that will work for those involved. You may have planned to teach a new worship chorus for the weekend, but due to a late start or musical difficulty, you save the new piece for another time. You may stay after rehearsal with one individual to solve a problem rather than make the entire group stay. It may require the director or other leaders in the group to make extra sacrifices. In contrast, there will be times when you know it is fine to rehearse longer than usual or to add additional time later in the week. If you acknowledge your awareness that everyone's time is sacred, then you will create the flexibility you need to modify time as necessary.

I am not proposing that you modify rehearsals each week by allowing people to "float in" when they see fit. You should expect people to be on time, educate them about the importance of punctuality, and plan the rehearsal as if they will be on time. There are particular instances where you cannot show flexibility; and you, as the clock of the group, decide when that is. Often, there will only be one person missing and you can certainly begin without them. My style, as one responsible for rehearsals, is to start rehearsing when everyone is present. With a two-hour rehearsal planned, my preference would be to rehearse two hours regardless of the starting time. However, I cannot let my personal preference make everyone else stand around and wait; nor can I keep everyone until all hours of the night. If the rehearsal director can see his or her task as being the "clock" of the group, rather than letting the clock control the group, then productivity will increase and frustration will decrease.

At this point in my experience, I still believe that there is hope for convincing every member of the ministry that "playing on time" only makes for a more enjoyable experience for all involved.

Rehearsal Cycles

Making sure rehearsals keep a sense of "new life" is important. If rehearsal simply becomes the "same old thing" every week, people will begin to lose the spark of excitement and joy needed for the ministry. Looking for patterns throughout the year will help you, as the rehearsal director, to shake things up when needed. With the rotational schedule discussed earlier, this often happens on its own. With a different group rehearsing each week, there is always a sense of newness in each rehearsal. Paying attention to how each individual interacts during rehearsal will help you to identify times when something out of the ordinary is needed. The ritual of rehearsal is where the actual music itself must come to life. However, half of the ritual is about the one leading the rehearsal providing an environment that allows for everyone to feel affirmed in living his or her gifts.

Chapter Seven
Facing the Music

There are so many issues in a music ministry that it is often the music that is taken for granted. Finding music and preparing music must be constantly balanced with your musicians' abilities and limitations, your congregation's abilities and limitations, and the copyright law. It would be easy to ignore the copyright law. In today's society, intellectual property is becoming increasingly difficult to protect, especially given the current Internet capabilities. However, you must make it a priority to follow the copyright law. Even as the technology makes it easier to ignore the law, the same technology will improve the system for detecting who is violating the law. Social interaction always finds a new balance between ownership and privacy, eventually. Do the right thing.

I have spent countless hours researching the way we format and prepare music for worship, what can and cannot be recorded for sale, and what can and cannot legally be used in worship. I have also hired a lawyer who specializes in copyright law to answer questions. On some issues his answers directly contradict what some people in contemporary Christian music circles are writing about the law. It is the responsibility of those in leadership to make the effort to follow the copyright law. I am grateful to be able to pay fees to companies such as CCLI, MPLC, (now offering CVLI), BMI, or ASCAP as they provide ways for churches to legally use other artists' work.

When someone calls to inquire about worship at my congregation, the question about resources generally arises. Where do you find music, drama, video clips, and so forth? I gladly share with them the resources we use, but I add this word of caution: We only use about 25 percent of all the resources that we search through. Music published by a well-known company does not necessarily fit our particular format.

Congregational Sensitivity

When a piece of music is used in a congregational setting, it should meet certain criteria. It must not only be musically appropriate, it must also be lyrically appropriate. It should also be something the musicians can play. Above all, it MUST be something the congregation can sink its teeth into. If the congregation cannot sing something, then what is the point? To know what your congregation can handle, you must assess its ability. What can the average person handle musically? I have no problems transposing a great song to a more appropriate key for congregational singing. You must try to provide music that allows the congregation to worship. There are some excellent new worship songs that our musicians love. We have used them as special pieces of music to connect with the message of the service. However, they will not be sung congregationally because they are too difficult for the congregation to sing. This statement is not meant to criticize the contemporary worship writers of the day, or to "dumb down" worship to kindergarten level. I place myself in this category, since some of the music I have written, assuming that it would work congregationally, has failed to do so. Instead, use such music in other creative ways.

Another way to be "in tune" with your congregation is to pay attention to them. There are so many different ways to do this. I have three worship services each weekend to assess how worship is "working." I may sit on the back row, the front row, or observe from the "loft" on the second floor. I may be singing or playing in the band. Wherever I am, there are a multitude of things to observe. When the congregation is singing, I pay close attention to their interaction with each song. There are times when music is chosen that we thought met all the criteria but failed miserably in worship. If, after a certain amount of time, a song is not working, we do not have a problem with taking it out of the congregational lineup. This is not something to regret, but rather something to learn. Figuring out why a particular song did not work helps one make better decisions for the future.

When we do choose new music for the congregation, we try to be very sensitive about how this music is introduced. We do not introduce a brand-new song during the time designated for congregational singing. There is an intentional pattern for teaching new music. As people gather before the service, we have a time of singing. We use the last song of this "pre-service" set as a place to teach a new worship chorus. Once we have "taught" the song for several weeks, we will then use it in the worship service. This pattern allows most people the opportunity to become familiar with the song before it becomes part of their worship time.

There are times when a piece of music will be used in a sermon series as a congregational response each week. These are usually repetitive in nature and shorter in length, often in Taizé style. When beginning a new series, we take time to teach this song to the congregation. However, it is still not done during congregational singing until people have had a chance to learn it.

It is also important to find a balance between the old, the new, and the favorites of the congregation. Currently, our worship format incorporates a different song each week from the denominational hymnal. We also include new music "of the day" that has become an "old favorite" in our congregation, with a constant effort to incorporate new, quality music just released from the publishing houses. At times I feel like a D.J. with more requests than airtime. Through prayer and an awareness of the theme of the service, I strive to make sure that the right music is presented each week.

"Special Music"

Where did the term "special music" originate? I have heard it used since childhood. It is that piece of music that the congregation generally does not sing. Many times it is the offertory. For my congregation, wherever it may fall in the service, it directly compliments and further ties in the message of the sermon. This music may be performed as a solo or by the entire band. It may be a Top 40 hit, a hymn, or a new worship chorus. It might finish out a drama or be woven into children's time. Whatever this music may be, *it is done in conjunc-*

tion with the theme of the service. There are those weeks throughout the year when no particular special music works any better than something that could be sung congregationally. When this is the case, we do not have "special music," but rather have an extended time of congregational singing.

What is *special* about "special music?" It is the connection made for those in the congregation and the opportunity for musicians to further live their gifts. It is not about someone performing or showcasing the musicians. This music provides the musicians a wide variety of musical experience, while allowing the congregation to experience another form of liturgy. As with dance, drama, or any other creative media, the special music is yet another creative way for people to express the love and grace of Christ and for the congregation to connect with God.

Stylistic Preference

As the director of a music ministry, your personal stylistic preference is a contributing factor to the musical repertoire of your ministry. This is not a negative thing. Musicians will naturally have stylistic preferences. The preferences and strengths of your musicians will contribute to the repertoire of your ministry as well. Music will be chosen according to your musician's ability level. The key is to not let anyone's personal style become a barrier to new growth.

In my particular situation, the stylistic variance of the musicians I work with is profound. It allows me to think in many different musical genres when searching for congregational and special music. Though my personal CD collection might seem very narrow to many, the collection of music I search through on a weekly basis is very broad. Part of my ability to do this comes from being stretched from one musical genre to another my entire life, as well as being taught the importance of diversity. I think it is crucial to stretch myself and the other musicians into new musical opportunities. There are times when the musicians think I have lost my mind when I hand out new music; but they are generally surprised and overjoyed in the end when all involved reach a new level of musical growth.

If you find yourself unexposed to a variety of styles, make it a priority to stretch and listen. Internet listening sites and local store listening stations make it very easy to become more aware of all the music that awaits your ministry. This may mean reusing a song from the '30s or using something released last week. It may mean using a song from the Celtic, Jazz, Classical, Rock, Country, Acoustic Soul or other musical genre. A good checklist for using a piece of music in your service might include:

- Is the music lyrically appropriate?
- Is it quality music that can be played by the musicians scheduled for the service?
- Will the music speak the "heart language" of those we are trying to reach?
- If the music is to be sung congregationally, is it "music level appropriate" for your congregation?

- If it is to be used as the "special music,"
  does it fit into the theme of the service in
  a way that will support and compliment
  the sermon and other creative elements?

Another excellent way to keep a fresh style in your ministry is to be receptive to other people's ideas. The creative ministry team is a great source for providing musical ideas. People in the congregation email suggestions. Also, the musicians within the ministry provide musical suggestions. They may offer a song suggestion that is not used, but in looking at the particular song, a door is opened to another piece of music. Every suggestion that is made in some way contributes to the search for music. It also may be the case that a suggested song might not surface for a year or more. By including the thoughts and ideas everyone brings to the table, the musical database is formed. The more diversity you embrace, the more depth your ministry contains.

Chapter Eight
The Journey to the Future

It was a crazy morning and the afternoon looked like it would be the same. I had someone coming to work on the sound system, a theory class to teach, and music to prepare for evening rehearsal. Checking the messages on my phone after a mad dash to Taco Bell, I was reminded that Ashley would be at the church soon.

Ashley is an amazing individual. If I am going out of town for a weekend, I know Ashley can take care of the multimedia responsibilities for worship. If needed, she can produce the service as well. She cannot recite her social security number, but the church's CCLI License Number is easily recalled. Ashley also has an amazing gift for both acting and music. Ashley is only thirteen.

Ashley was coming to the church that day because she wanted to learn to play the bass guitar. She sings in the youth band and plays piano, but the band is currently in need of a bass player. I knew Ashley would have no problem learning to play the bass. In a few hours she was already playing several of the songs the youth band is currently rehearsing. With lessons and continual practice, I anticipate Ashley will be playing with our adult bands before she is out of high school.

People in the church have worked with Ashley, and as a result, her gifts have grown. By participating in drama workshops and music workshops, and by being "my shadow," Ashley is building a foundation of creativity that will stay with her for the rest of her life. Ashley's creativity has been nurtured not only by the atmosphere of training provided by the church, but also by the support of her parents, private lessons, and other opportunities. She cannot imagine the doors that will be opened for her as she grows into all God would have her be.

The journey to the future begins with our children. We expect children to learn to read and speak properly, calculate accurately, and understand science and history. We should also expect great things from our children as they grow in their faith community. We, as leaders, must be able to see this dream into being. We should provide opportunities for children to play music as well as learn to read and speak the language of music. We should provide the opportunity for children to participate in drama and learn the skills and techniques associated with great actors. Children should also be allowed to experience technological and visual art through the eyes of great artists. These experiences also help children learn the "technique" of Christian community. By working together and learning to see the Light of Christ in each person, the children grow in their spiritual journey with a loving God. They are learning to become co-creators in God's Kingdom each and every day.

The Task at Hand

We must see it as our task to provide learning opportunities for future generations so they too will learn to live their gifts. Youth choir or youth handbell choir has been a place of participation and training for those under eighteen in many congregations. These are still wonderful ways for youth to participate in ministry and to learn musicality in the church. However, youth participating in churches with an adult band, or ministries such as multimedia, video, drama, creative movement, and visual art, also have a desire to participate in the same type of ministry on a youth level.

It is not always easy to help people "grow" their gifts. Training takes time and energy. Many people want music to be as instant as food from a fast food drive-in. I believe this is even more of an issue for our youth. They want instantly to sound like the hottest group on the radio. However, if we instill in them the idea that spiritual and musical growth is a lifelong process, then they will be more willing to commit to the journey. What must be avoided is giving them the idea that they are preparing for future "Gift Living." Children and youth should be actively involved in living their gifts in the present. Training is provided so that "Gift Living" becomes a way of life.

The Youth Band Format

In my congregation we do not have a youth choir in the traditional sense of the word, but all are welcome to participate in what we term the "youth band." They work on a rotational schedule similar to our adults. As their vocal section grows, we anticipate having a vocal ensemble setting for this group somewhat similar to that of our adult vocal ensemble. We also encourage our youth vocalists to sing with our adult vocal ensemble. They benefit from the experience of working with a group that is conducted. They gain many musical and team-building skills that carry over into their own band setting.

The most difficult part of dealing with a youth band is handling the range of ability. Often it would seem easier to divide the youth band into teams based on ability levels, but that cannot happen. An example from our "drum line" will explain why. The senior percussionist for the youth band could not keep a beat for four measures during his sophomore year. Now he plays with our youth and adult bands. He is studying with a local college percussion instructor and has a scholarship audition next month, hoping to major in percussion this fall. We have a seventh-grade drummer who six months ago would not play drums in front of people. He now "hangs" with our senior drummer. Having been on rotation with the more advanced youth musicians, his ability level has soared. The previous percussionist for the youth band is now in college and participates with our adult band. He was the stronghold of the youth percussion section while that "sophomore" was in training.

Several factors contributed to the growth of our percussionists, such as private lessons and the desire to learn. Another factor has been the direct support and encouragement of Brian, one of our adult percussionists. Brian serves as a mentor to our younger drummers, and in return, they respect him and appreciate his time and energy. Few people will spend the day "jammin'" in the worship area with nine sets and percussionists. Brian desires that everyone involved grow spiritually and musically. Both the adult and youth drummers enjoy many different styles of music and the challenge each piece of music presents. They also enjoy being together.

The drum line is one of our many examples of multi-generational ministry. Multigenerational ministry exists because of intentional emphasis on growing gifts at an early age. It also exists because we intentionally expose and incorporate those learning to live their gifts with those who are generations ahead. Brian's interaction with the youth has allowed musical and spiritual growth that would never have occurred if we had just sent them off for private lessons.

By combining youth with different levels of ability, younger ones can be intermingled with those who have had much more experience. This allows growth to occur in amazing ways. If we had told our seventh-grade drummer that he could play as soon as the senior graduates, then we would be starting from scratch next year. As with the adults, time and effort go into planning combinations of youth that work together to meet the needs of the service. It is crucial to have the right balance between stronger, senior high musicians and younger, less experienced ones.

As members of the youth team become high school juniors and reach the appropriate skill level, they are invited to rotate within our adult band. To keep this invitation, they must also continue to participate in the youth band while still in high school. This allows for yet another "growth spurt" as playing at the adult level stretches them. At present, we have three very talented musicians who moved from the youth band to the adult band. We have three seniors participating in both the youth and adult band. This is an intentional pattern. We have pianists, guitarists, vocalists, and other instrumentalists playing with all of the "old musicians" to create a strong line of growth.

Building Bridges of Support

Part of the support system that adults provide for the youth is to celebrate and encourage the style of worship our youth are doing within their specific ministry area. The youth have an important ministry as they lead worship in their department. The different ways they participate in living their gifts are simply different avenues of ministry. One is not superior to the other.

Our youth involved in music and drama had a special day this summer to work on new material. After working hard all day (and after some team-building activities that included eggs, flour, and gelatin), the youth band shared their accomplishments with the adult band "congregation." This is one of the ways we let the youth know we celebrate and support their ministry. We joke about "the old people" coming to hear them. The youth appreciate the support and have a great relationship with the adults. We are not just making connections; we are participating in growing the leaders of tomorrow.

The addition of a college intern has also provided an opportunity for growth in the youth band. The youth intern position mirrors my position in worship-related ministries providing similar coordination for youth services. The addition of this position has allowed for tremendous growth in the music ministry of the youth department.

A Multigenerational Mindset

At this point, some advocates of generationally target-ed worship might question this multigenerational approach. They argue that youth want to do a different style of music than an adult group. College-age students should be leading worship in their own style. This viewpoint is understandable for several dozen megachurches. If you are in a ministry that has enough staff to support separate worship services for each age group, and you choose to do that, you are blessed! But most people reading this chapter are not in that position. My congregation of 1,500 in worship cannot do it either. Most of my peers are at the point of trying to add a "new" type of service to the traditional services currently offered.

In our worship experiences, we try to provide a multi-generational balance in our non-traditional setting. I would not refer to our type of service as "blended." In fact, we think we are unique and not easily labeled. I plan for the seven-year-old as well as the seventy-year-old when working on a service. There are several families in our congregation who are three generations strong when they attend worship. Most people would find that odd in a church that only provides "contemporary worship," whatever that means. It is good for the seven-year-old to learn the hymns that have been part of our Christian heritage, and it is good for the seventy-year-old to learn the hymns of tomorrow. Both will be an important part of the younger generation's faith journey. Due to the multigenerational focus, our adult and youth music departments can relate. Our youth band and college ministries use some of the same music that our adult band plays. They also use some pieces you would not hear in a regular weekend service. *There is a place of intersection for all age groups, allowing individuality of worship as well as a time of combined worship.*

Ashley's Christmas present this year was a new bass. She is taking private lessons from one of our adult bassists. When I recently listened to her playing with the youth band, I was amazed at her progress. Afterwards, she spent the rest of the afternoon putting all of the music folders together for rehearsal while resting those tired bass fingers. Having her with me probably helped me more than it helped Ashley. She also prepared the PowerPoint presentation for the weekend services while she waited for her Mom to finish her own music rehearsal. God makes a way when we are listening to the call.

Are there members in your congregation that can help participate in training future generations? Is there someone who might see this as an exciting way of participating in building God's Kingdom for the future? Who are the children and youth around you with a gift yet to be discovered?

In Closing

After last weekend's service, an older gentleman came forward and waited to speak to me. As I walked over to him, he shook my hand and thanked me. He did not thank me because of the music, or the images in the PowerPoint presentation, or the beautiful altar created by the altar team, or for any of the other creative elements that had occurred in the worship service. He thanked me, very sincerely, for my smile.

Regardless of how the ministry changes along the journey, it is my hope that the joy this man saw in the ministry will never change. More than anything else, I want people to be touched by the love and grace of Christ through every service that is created. Though creative, quality ministry is always a goal, it is never a goal to be achieved by losing sight of the joy of ministry. Gift living is not about being "stuck" in the midst of the gifts you have been given. Gift living is about weaving the hearts of those in ministry together so that all the world sees is the love of Christ.

Appendix

References:

Gallwey, Timothy, and Green, Barry. *The Inner Game of Music* (Doubleday, 1986).

Ristad, Eloise. *A Soprano on Her Head* (Real People Press, 1982).

Sherbondy, Sharon. *Somebody's Got to Do It* (DM 9119) (Willow Creek Community Church, 1991).

Weber, Rob. *Visual Leadership: The Church Leader as ImageSmith* (Abingdon Press, Oct. 2002).

Weber, Rob. *ReConnecting: A Guide to the Wesleyan Renewal of Your Church* (Abingdon Press, Oct 2002).

Additional Resources:

See Chris and Carole Beatty's Vocal Coach resources on their website: http://www.vocalcoach.com/.

Find out about Will Denton at http://www.willdenton.com/.

Learn more about the ministries of Grace Community United Methodist Church on their website: http://www.gracehappens.org/

Printed in the United States
1483700001BA/70-75

9 780687 044214